FAVORITE TOYS

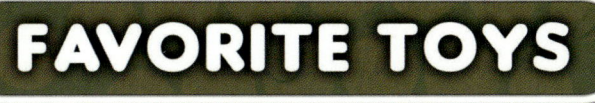

TOY CARS

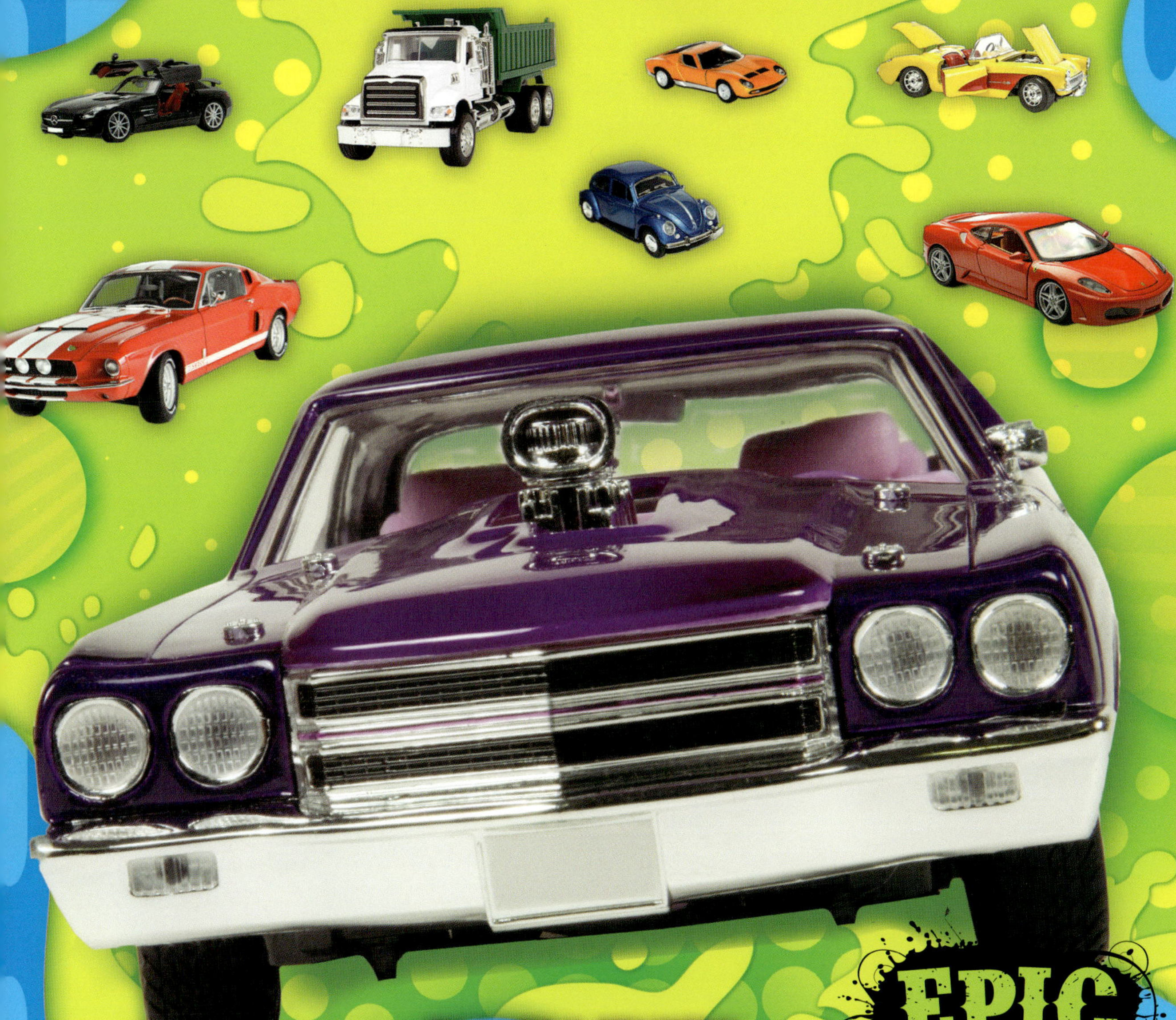

BY PAIGE V. POLINSKY

EPIC

BELLWETHER MEDIA • MINNEAPOLIS, MN

EPIC

Action and adventure collide in EPIC. Plunge into a universe of powerful beasts, hair-raising tales, and high-speed excitement. Astonishing explorations await. Can you handle it?

This edition first published in 2023 by Bellwether Media, Inc.

No part of this publication may be reproduced in whole or in part without written permission of the publisher. For information regarding permission, write to Bellwether Media, Inc., Attention: Permissions Department, 6012 Blue Circle Drive, Minnetonka, MN 55343.

Library of Congress Cataloging-in-Publication Data

LC record for Toy Cars available at: https://lccn.loc.gov/2022004840

Text copyright © 2023 by Bellwether Media, Inc. EPIC and associated logos are trademarks and/or registered trademarks of Bellwether Media, Inc.

Editor: Elizabeth Neuenfeldt   Designer: Josh Brink

Printed in the United States of America, North Mankato, MN.

TABLE OF CONTENTS

Need for Speed! 4
The History of Toy Cars 6
Toy Cars Today 14
More Than a Toy 20
Glossary 22
To Learn More 23
Index 24

Need for Speed!

Two toy cars zip along a twisting track. Ahead, the track lifts off the ground. It is a loop! The toy cars speed through it at full speed. They finish the race in record time!

The History of Toy Cars

Toy cars began in the early 1900s. The Dowst Brothers Company made **die-cast** toy cars.

TIN WHEELERS

TOYMAKERS IN NUREMBERG, GERMANY, BEGAN MAKING TINY TIN CARS IN THE 1900S. BUT THEY BROKE EASILY.

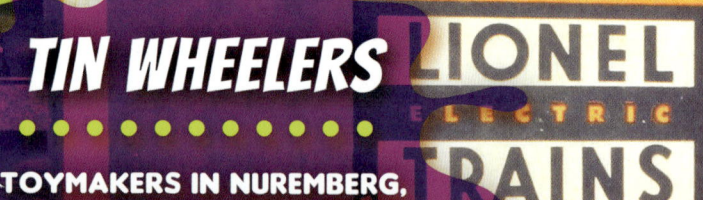

TOY CAR BEGINNINGS

Dowst Brothers Company: Chicago, Illinois = 🔴

Lionel Corporation: New York City, New York = 🔵

Around this time, the Lionel **Corporation** made **electric** toy cars. Each set had two toy cars and a track.

More companies made die-cast cars. In 1952, Jack Odell made the first Matchbox car for his daughter. It was a tiny steamroller. Lesney Products started selling Matchbox cars in 1953. They were simple and hard to break. People loved them!

JACK ODELL

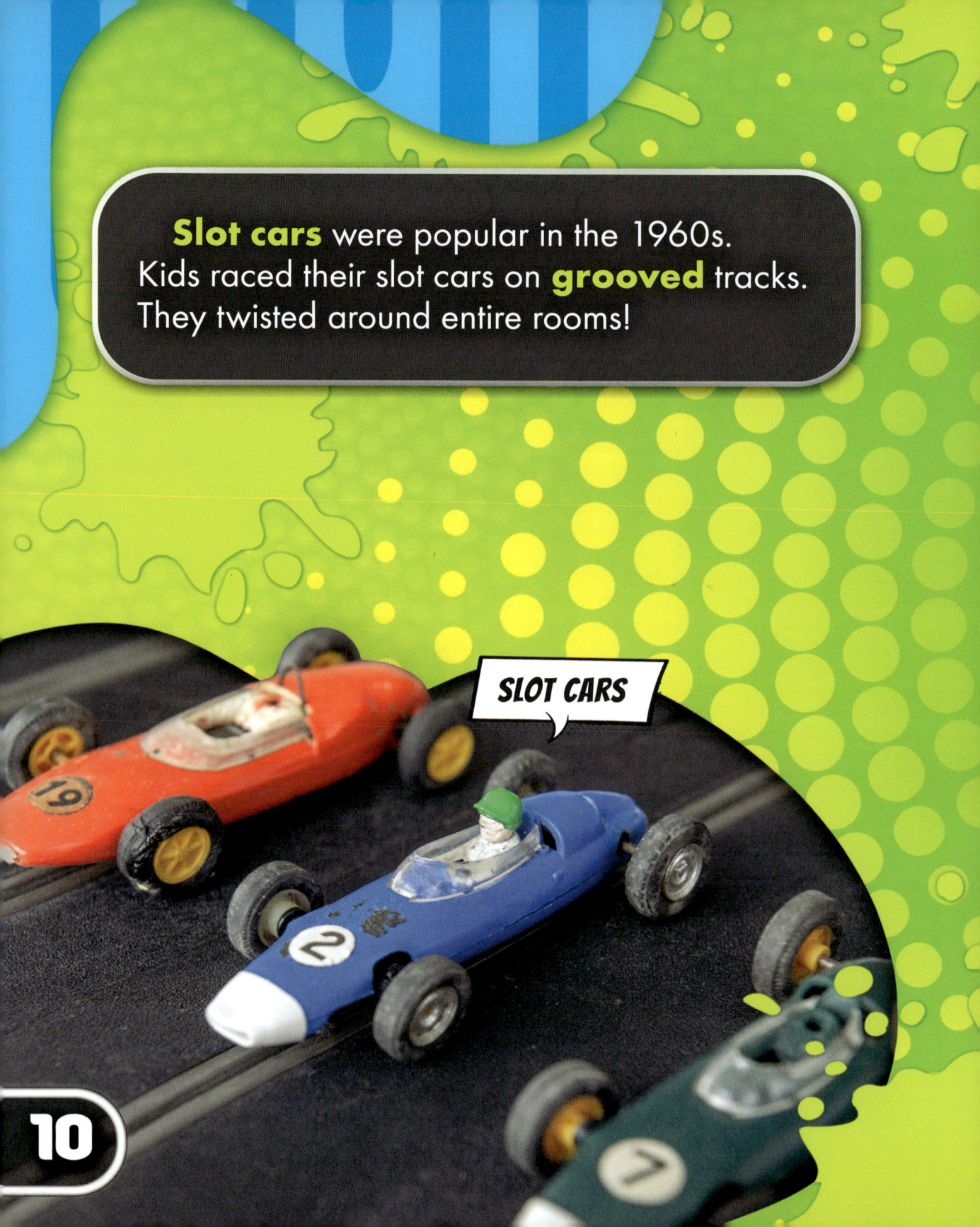

Slot cars were popular in the 1960s. Kids raced their slot cars on **grooved** tracks. They twisted around entire rooms!

SLOT CARS

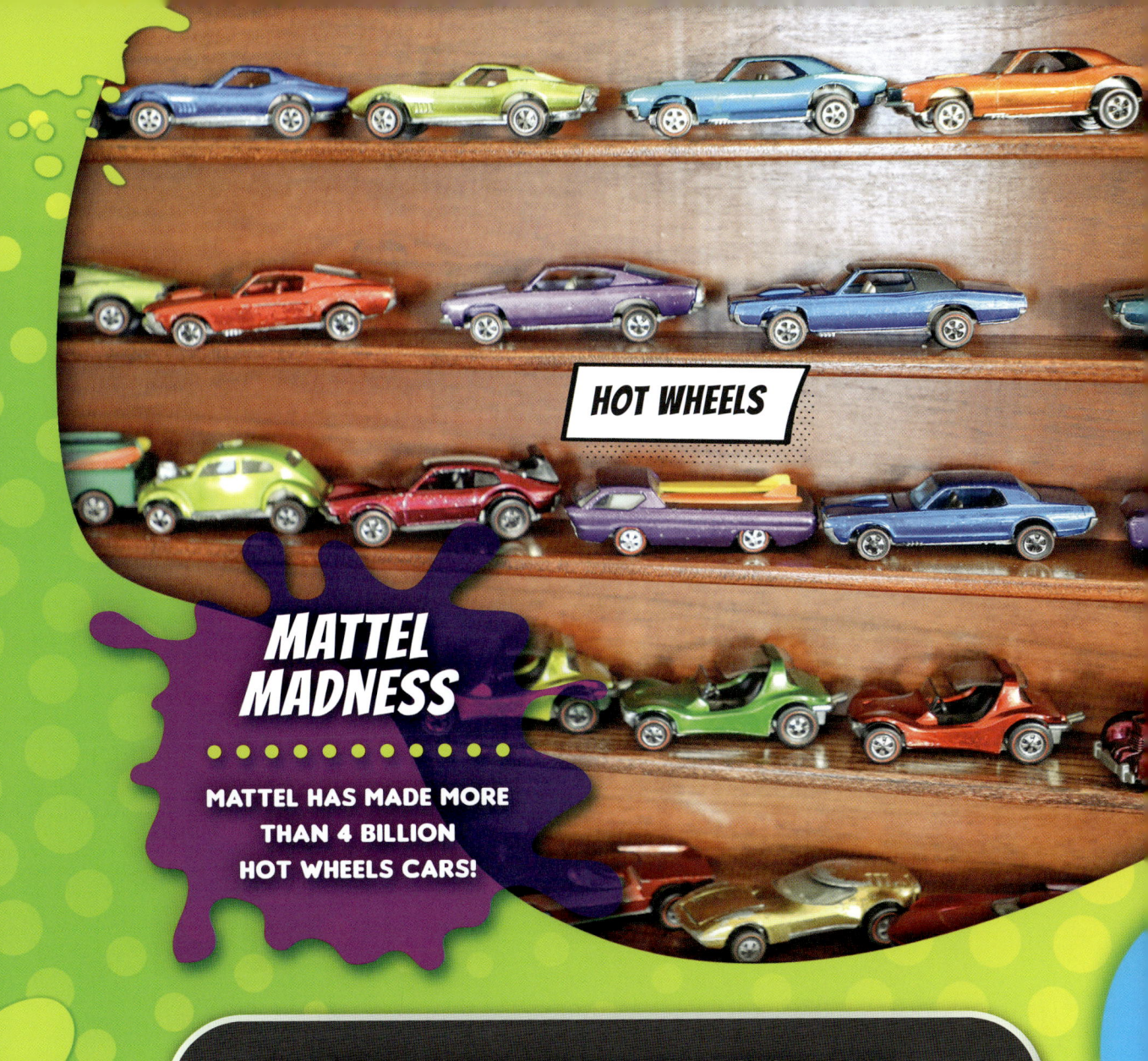

HOT WHEELS

MATTEL MADNESS

MATTEL HAS MADE MORE THAN 4 BILLION HOT WHEELS CARS!

In 1968, Mattel introduced die-cast Hot Wheels. Mattel also sold track pieces. Kids could build their own racetracks!

By the 1970s, **RC cars** started to become popular. These cars worked on any smooth road! **Off-road** RC cars came with special tires. Some made sounds and had lights!

RC CARS

TOY CAR TIMELINE

early 1900s
The Dowst Brothers Company makes die-cast toy cars

1912
The Lionel Corporation releases the first electric toy cars

1953
Lesney Products starts selling Matchbox cars

1968
Mattel starts selling Hot Wheels

13

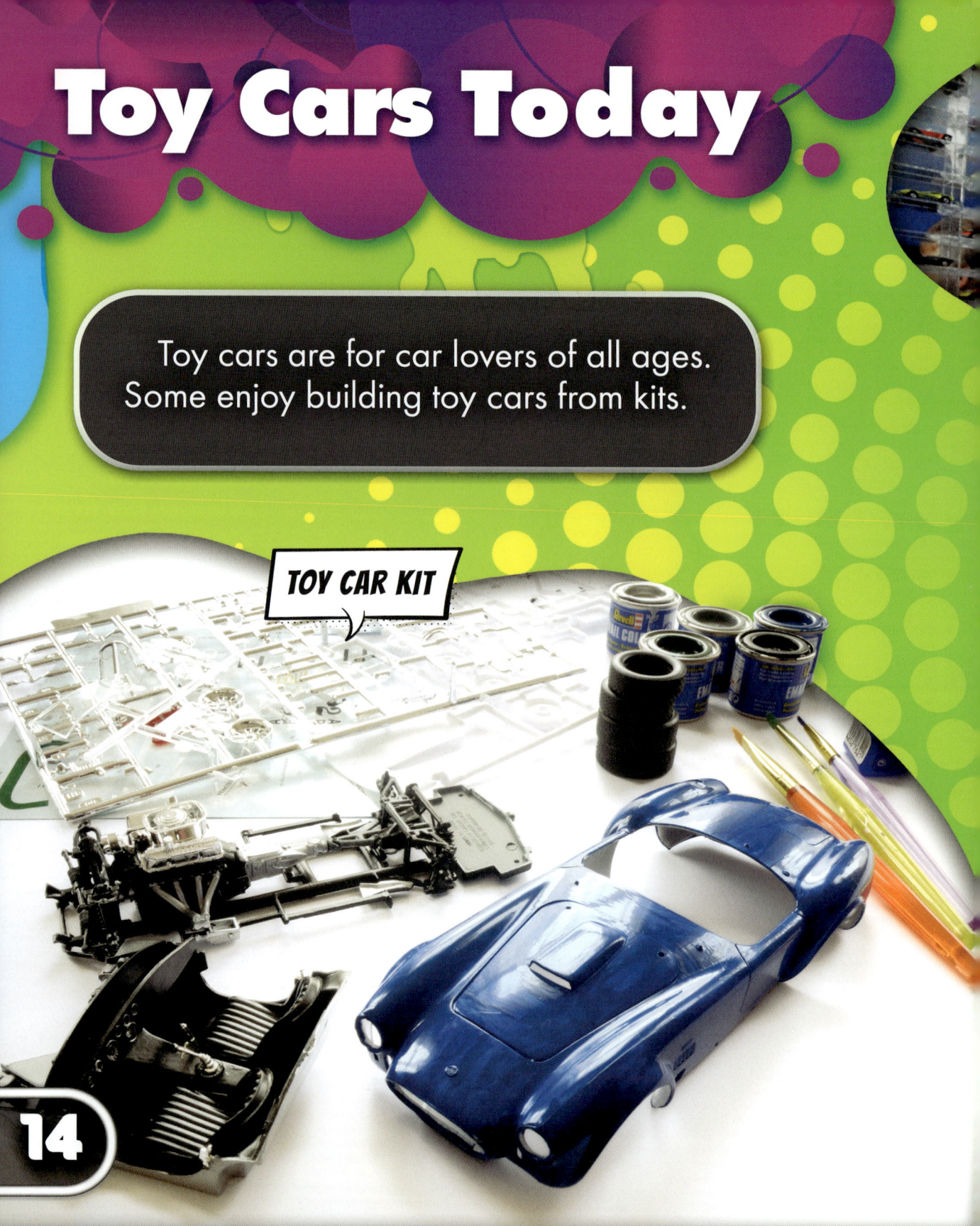

Toy Cars Today

Toy cars are for car lovers of all ages. Some enjoy building toy cars from kits.

TOY CAR KIT

HOT WHEELS COLLECTOR

TOP COLLECTOR

NABIL KARAM OF LEBANON HOLDS THE WORLD RECORD FOR BIGGEST TOY CAR COLLECTION. HE OWNS 37,777 DIFFERENT CARS!

Adults like to collect the cars they played with as kids. Older cars can be very **valuable**!

Many toy cars are based on movies, TV shows, and video games.

Other toys look like real cars. Mattel makes Matchbox cars based on electric and **hybrid** cars!

TOY CAR TYPES

Hot Wheels

Matchbox

LEGO Speed Champions

Hasbro Micro Machines

RC cars are faster than ever. Some race up to 100 miles (161 kilometers) per hour!

SLOT CAR RACING

STILL SLOTTING

Today, there are around 200 slot car raceways in the United States.

There are also different kinds of RC cars. Some are race cars. Others are monster trucks!

More Than a Toy

Today, fans play games like *Hot Wheels Open World* on **Roblox**. Collectors meet up at the **Annual** Matchbox Collector's Show. There are many ways to enjoy toy cars!

HOT WHEELS OPEN WORLD ON ROBLOX

ANNUAL MATCHBOX COLLECTOR'S SHOW PROFILE

What Is It? An event where fans celebrate and sell Matchbox cars

Where Is It? The AACA Museum in Hershey, Pennsylvania

When Does It Happen? Once a year

AACA MUSEUM

Glossary

annual—happening once a year

corporation—a business or organization

die-cast—formed by pouring melted metal into a mold

hybrid—relating to something that is made of two different things

electric—relating to electricity; electricity is a form of energy that is carried through wires and is used to power things such as machines and lights.

grooved—having a long, thin cut in a surface

off-road—used on trails or dirt roads

RC cars—remote control cars; remote controls are devices that can control something else from a distance.

Roblox—a website and app where people can play games created by other users

slot cars—toy racing cars that are electric and have a part that lets them move along grooved tracks

valuable—worth a lot of money

To Learn More

AT THE LIBRARY

Cannons, Helen Cox. *The History of Toys*. Oxford, U.K.: Raintree, 2020.

Sommer, Nathan. *Nerf Blasters*. Minneapolis, Minn.: Bellwether Media, 2022.

Storm, Marysa. *Formula 1 Cars*. Mankato, Minn.: Black Rabbit Books, 2020.

ON THE WEB

FACTSURFER

Factsurfer.com gives you a safe, fun way to find more information.

1. Go to www.factsurfer.com.

2. Enter "toy cars" into the search box and click 🔍.

3. Select your book cover to see a list of related content.

Index

adults, 15
Annual Matchbox Collector's Show, 20, 21
beginnings, 7
collect, 15, 20
die-cast, 6, 8, 11, 16
Dowst Brothers Company, 6
electric, 7, 17
history, 6, 7, 8, 10, 11, 12
Hot Wheels, 11, 15, 16, 20
Hot Wheels Open World, 20
Karam, Nabil, 15
kids, 10, 11, 15
kits, 14
Lesney Products, 8
Lionel Corporation, 7
Matchbox car, 8, 9, 17
Mattel, 11, 17
Odell, Jack, 8
RC cars, 12, 18, 19
Roblox, 20
slot cars, 10, 19
timeline, 13
tin cars, 6
track, 4, 7, 10, 11
types, 17

The images in this book are reproduced through the courtesy of: Dana Kenneth Johnson, cover (hero); CTRPhotos, cover (top left blue car), pp. 17 (Hot Wheels), 21 (yellow car top); Andrey Lobachev, cover (top left black car), back cover (top right, bottom right); Zlajs, cover (bottom left red car); fotosv, cover (top white truck), p. 3 (bottom); MaximKir, cover (top middle orange car); Nurlan Mammadzada, cover (middle blue car); urbanbuzz, cover (top right yellow car); Hetman Bohdan, cover (red right middle); charles taylor, back cover (top left); oculo, back cover (bottom left); Pelikh Alexey, p. 2 (top); andesseot, p. 2 (bottom); Smlyubov, p. 4; Semmick Photo, pp. 4-5 (children); Alan Mognet/ Alamy, p. 6; Stan Meagher/ Stringer/ Getty Images, p. 8; Chris Ware/ Stringer/ Getty Images, p. 9 (top); Chris Wilson/ Alamy, pp. 9 (bottom), 13 (bottom); Phil Rees/ Alamy, p. 10; Curt DeWolff/ Alamy, p. 11; INTERFOTO/ Alamy, p. 12; mjwman/ Alamy, p. 13 (top); Tim Jones/ Alamy, p. 14; MediaNews Group/ Orange County Register/ Getty Images, p. 15; Shyripa Alexandr, p. 16 (Star Wars); Kociboy, p. 16 (Iron Man); Kik Sam, p. 16 (Jurassic Park); Gabor Mika, p. 17 (Matchbox); Ekaterina Minaeva, p. 17; JHPhoto/ Alamy, p. 17; Zaruba Ondrej, p. 18; BearFotos, p. 19; karakedi35, p. 20 (laptop); Elizabeth Neuenfeldt/ Bellwether Media, p. 20 (screen); Walter Bibikow/ DanitaDelimont.com/ Alamy, p. 21; windu_dolan, p. 22; Mikhail Zyablov, p. 23.